SEA STARS

ANIMALS WITHOUT BONES

Jason Cooper

Rourke Publications, Inc.
Vero Beach, Florida 32964

PHOTO CREDITS
© Lynn M. Stone: cover, page 4, 10, 15, 18, 21; © Breck Kent:
title page, pages 8, 17; © Herb Segars: pages 7, 13;
© Alex Kirstitch: page 12

Library of Congress Cataloging-in-Publication Data
Cooper, Jason, 1942-
    Sea stars / by Jason Cooper.
        p. cm. — (Animals without bones)
    Includes index.
    Summary: A simple introduction to the physical characteristics,
life cycle, and habitat of starfish and related species.
    ISBN 0-86625-569-9
    1. Starfishes—Juvenile literature. [1. Starfishes.] I. Title.
II. Series: Cooper, Jason, 1942-   Animals without bones.
QL384.A8C68   1996
593.9'3—dc20   95-26011
                                        CIP
                                        AC

Printed in the USA

TABLE OF CONTENTS

SEA STARS

Many sea stars — or starfish — have five "arms," so they look like five-pointed stars. Sea stars are not really stars, of course, nor are they fish.

Sea stars belong to a family of simple, boneless animals called **echinoderms** (ee KIY no dermz).

Sea stars can look quite stiff and flat, like cookies with arms. However, the arms of sea stars can twist and bend like fingers.

Sea stars can bend and twist to get
a grip on things

WHAT SEA STARS LOOK LIKE

Not every **species** (SPEE sheez), or kind, of sea star has five arms. Some have six arms and others have almost 50! Even the species that usually have five arms may have fewer or more than five.

A sea star's arms reach out from a center, like spokes on a wheel. The top of the arms feels like rough sandpaper.

This young diver has a pair of five-armed sea stars from the sea floor

KINDS OF STARFISH

Starfish come in many kinds and colors. In fact, about 1,800 different kinds of starfish live in the oceans of the world. Starfish may be orange, red, blue, purple, yellow, or brown. Sometimes starfish of the same kind have different colors.

Many kinds of sea stars live along the ocean coasts of North America. One of the most colorful is the blood star.

The blood star is one of the most colorful echinoderms

THE SEA STAR FAMILY

All of the sea stars and their echinoderm cousins are **marine** (muh REEN), or sea, animals. Scientists have found about 6,500 kinds of echinoderms.

Sand dollars and sea urchins are well-known echinoderms. Sand dollars have a coat of tiny, hairlike spines. Most sea urchins have long, sharp spines.

Other members of the family include brittle stars, basket stars and sea cucumbers. Sea cucumbers look like pickles.

Sea urchins are like spiny sea stars   11
without arms

The crown of thorns sea star feeds on huge colonies of coral in the Indian Ocean

The spiny sun star is a northern species, living up into the Arctic

WHERE SEA STARS LIVE

Sea stars live in the oceans, warm and cold. Some species make their homes in the icy Antarctic Ocean!

Each species has its own favorite **habitat** (HAB uh tat), or kind of home. Ochre stars of the Pacific, for example, cling to rocks along the coast. People can see them easily when the ocean **tide** (TIYD) is low. Other types of sea stars like deeper water or a sandy ocean bottom.

Low tide on the Oregon coast shows an ochre sea star on rocks

BABY SEA STARS

Baby sea stars begin life as soft, tiny creatures called **larvas** (LAR vuhz). New larvas don't look much like adult starfish. Larvas go through changes as they grow in the ocean. Only when they are fully grown do they look like sea *stars*.

Some sea stars can grow another sea star by breaking off an arm! The "lost" arm grows into a whole new sea star.

Starfish live for about three to five years.

Having lost an arm, this sea star is growing a new one

HOW SEA STARS LIVE

Sea stars aren't quick, but they do get around. A sea star may travel in the sea by forcing water through its body.

Some species use the tips of their arms as walking "feet." A sea star's "real" feet are tiny suckers that hold onto rocks and food.

The rows of tiny orange feet on the underside of this sea star help it move and grip

PREDATOR AND PREY

Sea stars have poor senses, but they are good **predators** (PRED uh torz), or hunters. They eat mostly clams, mussels, and oysters. They also eat sea anemones, worms, sponges, and other sea stars.

A clam doesn't just open up its shell for a sea star. The sea star attaches its hundreds of tubed feet to the clammed-up clam. The little feet pull and pull until the clam gets tired and the shell opens. Then the sea star eats the soft parts of the clam.

Starfish are sometimes **prey** (PRAY), or food, for gulls and other larger animals.

A common Atlantic sea star preys on a favorite food, the mussel clam

SEA STARS AND PEOPLE

Most sea stars don't hurt people. The crown of thorns sea star, however, has sharp spines that can cause painful cuts. This star is common in the coral reefs of the Indian Ocean.

People often find sea stars in rocky tide pools at low tide. One of the best places to find them is along the coast of the Northwest.

Dry, dead starfish that wash ashore are great souvenirs (soo veh NEERZ), or keepsakes, of the sea.

Glossary

echinoderm (ee KIY no derm) — a group of small, boneless sea animals, including urchins, sea stars, sea cucumbers, and others

habitat (HAB uh tat) — the special kind of place where an animal lives, such as the sandy bottom of a warm, shallow *sea*

larva (LAR vuh) — an early stage of life in some animals; the young animal does not look like the adult it will become

marine (muh REEN) — of or relating to the sea and salt water

predator (PRED uh tor) — an animal that kills other animals for food

prey (PRAY) — an animal that is killed by another animal for food

species (SPEE sheez) — within a group of closely-related animals, one certain kind, such as an *ochre* star

tide (TIYD) — the daily rise and fall of the ocean caused by the moon's gravity, or pull

INDEX